# Rooroo, the Rooster

## By Joy Cowley

Illustrated by Jane Molineaux

🔂 Dominie Press, Inc.

Publisher: Christine Yuen
Editor: John S. F. Graham
Designer: Lois Stanfield
Illustrator: Jane Molineaux

Published by:

**ⓔ Dominie Press, Inc.**

1949 Kellogg Avenue
Carlsbad, California 92008 USA

www.dominie.com

Paperback ISBN 0-7685-1072-4
Library Bound Edition ISBN 0-7685-1489-4
Printed in Singapore
  3 4 5 6 7 8      09 08 07 06

# Table of Contents

## Chapter One

# Alarm Clock

At six in the morning,
winter and summer,
Rooroo, the rooster,
flew to the roof
of the Cackleberry henhouse
and crowed to wake up the town.

"Roo-a-roo-roo-roo!"

Lights went on in the houses.
Curtains were pulled back.
Showers ran hot.
Coffee and toast were made.

"Roo-a-roo-roo-roo!"

The bus driver started her bus.
The teacher picked up his milk.
The shopkeepers came out
in their pajamas
to get their newspapers
and look at the weather.

At the Cackleberry farm,
the farmer took a bucket
of food to the chickens.
"We don't need an alarm clock
with you here," she said to Rooroo.

## Chapter Two

# Slobber, the Puppy

**O**ne afternoon, Rooroo
was scratching under an oak tree.
His fine feathers were flying
like flags in the breeze.

Rooroo didn't see
Slobber, the puppy, behind him.
Slobber pounced and grabbed
some tail feathers in her teeth.

What a fright that rooster got!
Feathers and oak leaves
flew up in a storm.

Slobber, the puppy, ran away
with two of Rooroo's tail feathers
in her mouth.

Rooroo opened his beak to yell,
but no yell came out.
He tried again and again.
The only sound he could make
was a faint croak.
"I've lost my voice!" he whispered.

The hens gathered around him.

"It's shock," said Agatha.
"Sit down and have a rest."

"Wrap a cabbage leaf
around your throat,"
said Sybil Hen.

"Try a glass of slug juice,"
said Lulu.

Chapter Three

# A Frog in a Flour Sack

**A**t six the next morning,
Rooroo sat on the roof
and flapped his wings.

"Croak-a-roo-roo-roo!"

He opened his beak wider
and tried harder.

"Croak-a-roo-roo-roo!"

All the hens except Sybil Hen
went on sleeping.
"Your poor father!"
she said to her chicks.
"He sounds like a frog
in a flour sack."

## Chapter Four

# A Frantic Rushing

The sun rose high over the town,
and all the people kept sleeping.
When they did wake up,
there was a frantic rushing
here and there.

"What happened?" people cried,
as they pulled clothes on
over their pajamas
and burned their toast.
The bus was late.
School was late.
The shops did not open
until eleven o'clock.

"What happened to that rooster?"
everyone wanted to know.

It was lunchtime
when the farmer woke up.
The bucket of food came very late,
and the hens were hungry.

"Rooroo!" snapped Agatha.
"Do something about your voice!"

"I can't," whispered Rooroo,
who was too unhappy to eat.

## Chapter Five

# Open Your Beak!

**A**ll that day, Rooroo, the rooster,
moped in the Cackleberry henhouse,
his voice as weak
as a new chicken's cheep.

Late that night,
Sybil Hen went to the corner
where Rooroo sat.

"Open your beak!" she clucked.

Sybil Hen put her beak
into Rooroo's mouth
and looked down his throat.

Then she pulled out
something big and hard,
and spat it on the ground.

"That's your trouble," she said.
"You had an acorn in your throat."

Rooroo swallowed.
Then he put his head back
and tried his voice.

*Roo-a-roo-roo-roo!*

*Roo-a-roo-roo-roo!"*

## Chapter Six

# You'll Get It Right

**A**ll over town,

the lights went on.

People jumped out of bed.

Showers ran hot.

Coffee and toast were made.

But no one could understand
why the sky was still covered
with stars.

A sleepy farmer
came to the henhouse
with buckets of food.
She didn't know
that it was midnight.

Sybil Hen clucked at Rooroo.
"Don't worry, dear," she said.
"You'll get it right."